Praise for *The Accidental Observer*

The poetry reading community owes a huge debt of gratitude to Lola Koundakjian for her years of service to the art, making the work of Armenian poets, writers of Armenian ancestry in many languages, available to readers world-wide with her *Armenian Poetry Project*. Now, we meet Lola herself in three languages…and it's about time!

— *Diana Der-Hovanessian*

Lola Koundakjian's first collection reveals a curious and prescient mind roaming the landscapes of our collective illusions – and disillusionments. Through her spare style and a measured economy of language, she manages to decipher the banality of the everyday on one page, and, on the next, dissect the anatomy of suffering. Insightful and poignant, this is the work of a meticulous observer, and an acutely aware consciousness.

— *Amir Parsa*

These poems of longing and grace are the kind we pass from friend to friend. How wonderful to find them in three languages, each proclaiming their own bright joy.

— *William Michaelian*

These poems tread lightly but so perceptively. In delicate language and in three tongues, the poet takes us on a winding journey, a walk through "the dew intertwined with mist" on the path leading to and from love, to and from a lover who is now there, now absent. This theme is played out sensitively against backdrops of New York, with echos of the Middle East and Armenia sounding *sotto voce*. A vignette of a garden on West 87th street with a mulberry tree and "crushed ripe mulberries" evokes loss, love and childhood. From this miniature of New York, Koundakjian shows us far places freshly — Firenze and Toscana, afternoon coffee in Spain and an evocation of Morocco. The Armenian and English texts are transpositions of her perceptions into the different cultures, each rewarding in its own modality and in the meaning to be found in the place between them.

— *Michael E. Stone*

"y desapareces/ dejándome recuerdos/ bocados apenas" así inicia Lola Koundakjian su potencia evocadora. Así, dando nombres a los gestos íntimos de un pasado que se le hace pedazos en la memoria. Así, sus poemas, como un libro de viajes, recorren las sensaciones en imágenes que agregan futuro a lo ya sucedido. Olores, sabores y miradas que conforman memoriales cuyo objetivo es transformar el espacio de escritura en espacio conmemorativo. La densidad de Koundakjian reside en ofrecer ternura a la resistencia, en acordar una cita agradecida con sus raíces produciendo su propia perpetuación. El rito de la palabra hace justicia, nombra el destino del poema junto a su lector; su calidad de testigo.

— *Ana Arzoumanian*

Lola Koundakjian continues to open doors with her passion for poetry. These spare but heartfelt pieces have several faces and textures because of the work she has done with their translations. An ambitious project that only a poetry advocate such as Lola can deliver.

— *Armine Iknadossian*

Lola Koundakjian goes after real moments, and she does so quickly, concisely, masterfully--as if she is in panic of losing that rare afternoon light or the playful shadows cast over Central Park by the accidental cumulus clouds. She's like those rare poet-photographers that must work swiftly if they want to capture the moment just right.

— *Shahé Mankerian*

Lola Koundakjian

The Accidental Observer

Քերթուածներ / POESIAS

New York
2011

The Accidental Observer

ՔԵՐԹՈՒԱԾՆԵՐ / POESIAS

Second printing, October 2011

Copyright © 2011 R.H. Lola Koundakjian
Publisher ARMENIAN POETRY PROJECT

NoMAA Regrant Program, made possible by the JPMorgan Chase Foundation and the Upper Manhattan Empowerment Zone Development Corporation
All rights reserved
Published in the United States.

ISBN:978-0-578-06618-9
Armenian text edited by Maroush Yeramian
Spanish translations by *León Blanco* except where noted.
Cover design by Karen Cattan, *Sugarstudio*
Cover photo *Musée D'Orsay* by R.H. Lola Koundakjian

Ի յիշատակ մեծմօրս Էօժենի Քէօշկերեանին
եւ
ի յարգանք իր դուստրերուն՝
Այտա (մայրս), Անահիտ եւ Սօնիա Փոյատեաններուն

ACKNOWLEDGEMENT

Some of these poems have appeared online in *alpialdelapalabra* (Argentina), *Armenian Poetry Project* (New York City), *GROONG* (University of Southern California), *Mediterannean.nu*, and, *UniVerse* (Chicago); and in print in the Anthology *Memoria del XX Festival Internacional de Poesía de Medellin* (Colombia) *Armenian Weekly* (Boston, USA) and *Pakin* (Beirut, Lebanon).

Many thanks to NoMAA, Nancy Agabian of *GARTAL*, Amir Parsa, Ana Arzoumanian, Léon Blanco, Diana Der-Hovanessian, Armine Iknadossian, Shahé Mankerian, William Michaelian, Esteban Moore, Pamela Ospina, Alan Semerdjian, Michael E. Stone, Sotère Torregian, Alan Whitehorn, Maroush Yeramian.

A special thanks to the poets and people I met in Medellín Colombia.

ԲՈՎԱՆԴԱԿՈՒԹԻՒՆ
Contents/Contenido

1. ԱՇԱ ՀԱՍԱՆՔ ԱՄԱՌՈՒԱՆ ՍԿԻԶԲԸ/ And so, it is the beginning of summer/ Y es el principio del verano
2. ԱՇՈՒՆ/Fall/Otoño
3. ԵՐԿՈՒ ԱՆԽՆԵՐ/ The Two Anis/ Las dos Anis
4. ԹԹԵՆԻՆ/ The Mulberry Tree/ La Morera
5. Ի ՅԻՇԱՏԱԿ ՄՈՌԱՑՈՒԹԵԱՆ/ To the memory of forgetfulness/ A la memoria del olvido
6. ԿԵԱՆՔ/ Life (English version)/ Vida
7. ՆՍՏԱԾ ԵՄ/ Sitting/ Me siento
8. ՊՈՍՏՈՆ/ Boston/ Boston
9. ԱՆՁՐԵՒ/Rain/ Lluvia
10. ԳԻՇԵՐԸ/ Evening/ Al atardecer
11. ՏԱՍԸ/Ten/ Diez
12. ԳԱԼՈՎ ԱՆՑԵԱԼԷՆ/ Speaking of the Past/ Hablando del pasado
13. Manifesto/ Manifesto/Manifiesto
14. ՏԱՊԱՆԱՔԱՐ/ Tombstone/ Lápida
15. ՁՕՆ/ Ode/ Oda
16. ՄԱԶԵՐԴ/ Your hair/Tu cabello
17. ԳԻՇԵՐԸ ՔՈՒՆԻՍ ՄԷՋ / As I sleep/ Mientras duermo
18. ԼՈՒՍՆԱԿ ԳԻՇԵՐ Է/ It is a moonlit sky/ Es un cielo iluminado
19. Karaoke-ԱԿԱՆ ԱՆԷԾՔՆԵՐ/ Karaoke curses/ Maldiciones de Karaoke
20. ԿԻՐԱԿԻ ԱՌՏՈՒ/ Sunday Morning/ Mañana de Domingo
21. I wore white/ Escribí blanco
22. Six Balloons/ Seis globos
23. Vin Santo/ Vino Santo
24. Three cups of Heaven/ Tres tazas de cielo
25. My new bookcases/ Mis nuevas bibliotecas
26. Music/ Música
27. ԱՆՈՆՔ ՄԵՌԱՆ/ They died/ Murieron

Foreword

A subway ride from Washington Heights to the summit of Mt. Ararat
For Lola Koundakjian

My songs like the centuries have reached those wide banks of the world to come.
Eghishé Charents

Je tiens le flot de la rivière comme un violon.
I hold the tide of the river like a violin
Paul Eluard, *Donner à voir.*

"Where do I begin?" That's the phrase I would use to describe the path of *Le Merveilleux* — the Marvelous — that led me to Lola Koundakjian and her poetry.

Had it not been for my dear departed friends, Lemyel and Queenie Amirian, whom I met in the 1960's, introduced to me by their lovely daughter, Lorraine Amirian-Parker, I believe this odyssey might never have happened, — for *me*, that is to say. The Amirians urged me to meet their poet friend, Archie. "You'll love Archie", they said, "you'll find that you both have a lot in common the way you view life". As it so happened I did not get to meet Archie — Khatchig Minasian — until some years later. By another nudge of the Marvelous, we became neighbors on Emerson Street in Palo Alto, CA. I was by then a single parent, living with my teenage daughters and my aged mother.

From our first meeting I loved Archie as a friend and brother as well as fellow poet. He shared innumerable stories and anecdotes about his cousin, Willie — William Saroyan — the most memorable being, "It was me, *I* encouraged Willie to write; I helped him with his first poems!"

Archie constantly alluded to boxes of "Willie's early writings" which he had preserved in his garage. I continually cajoled Archie: "Let's have a reading together", as I had given a number of readings from my books in the 1980's in San Francisco, as well as

Stanford where I had been a lecturer. But Archie balked, saying he was no longer interested in public appearances.

In 1985, Archie passed away, stricken with cancer. I still see his Fedora hat and puffing cigar coming along the alleyway fence that ran along our old neighborhood; I can still hear his basso voice, his laugh, and his crazy jokes, which always lifted our spirits in difficult days.

And here's my link to Lola Koundakjian. She, too, loves Archie, although never having met him. It was through his poetry that she felt kinship with this wonderful poet — and here began my kinship with Lola. Archie's memory was a kind of bridge for us to meet, where our friendship has grown over the past two years. We have exchanged poems and letters through the post. I cannot say how much Lola's friendship has enriched my life with her stories and memories. She brings to me again, this lovely poet, the panoply of Armenia, which to me is itself the substance of poetry, each time we speak.

Armenia and its history, in particular the Armenian Genocide, still denied today by the Turkish government whose Ottoman predecessors committed this atrocity, are always in my mind. I continue to see the nameless faces of Armenian men, women and children in the Long March of Van. I have vowed as long as it is in my power that they will not be forgotten or be relegated into oblivion. Through Lola's work their cries come to the fore, through the marvel of her poetry.

Our ways are very different: I am, as I designate myself, a French Surrealist poet in America; Lola is a stylist, concerned with metrics, craft and *meaning* in her work. As for race, she is fully Armenian; I am not: I am amongst those William Saroyan embraced stating even with $1/16^{th}$ Armenian blood we can still feel a vital bond and love for Armenia, her people, culture, poetry and her destiny. Through my blood runs the lineage of Moors, Arabs, Greeks, Byzantines and even Ethiopic forebears, from the Island of Sicily, but my fascination with Armenia and things Armenian began when I was a teenager and has lasted fifty years.

Armenia's destiny has been embodied in her early poets, the *Ashoughs* and their tradition continues throughout its Diaspora — its language, music and liturgy. One of my French Surrealist *compères*, Benjamin Peret, in his *Anthologie de l'Amour sublime*, 1956, included a substantial number of Armenian *Ashoughs*. Diana Der-Hovanessian, later translated Armenian poets for her ANTHOLOGY OF ARMENIAN POETRY (1979).

Traditionally *Ashoughs* have been men, but I say now that precedent has been broken in Women poets of Armenian background… I proclaim Lola Koundakjian as *Ashough*, a Woman *Ashough*! – of whom my old friend Archie Minasian would be proud. He rightfully should have been writing this forward, were he still with us. I take it on with all humility and *hommage* to this wonderful poet that the Marvellous "out of the blue" has manifested unto me.

Coming from a Surrealist background and *esthétique*, I am less concerned with a poet's verse structure as with the verve, the spirit of the work -- *l'esprit de la poésie* – the dreams, the conviction, the *puissance* — le *cri* (which can be roughly be translated from the French as the dynamic of the voice, the cry if you will). It is this, which resonates with me, no matter how our respective conceptions of ideologies of poetry, may differ.

I can say I have only to read a few lines and then I *know* whether or not I feel a *connection* with this writer. Thus I can say I feel very *connected* with what Lola Koundakjian writes, with every line, with every poem she has sent to me.

And for me, she helps to expand the variegated life of poetry that continues to infuse the horizon of this world.

Sotère Torregian
August, AD 2010, Stockton, California

1.

Ահա հասանք ամառուան սկիզբը
եւ դուն կ'անհետանաս
ինձի թողնելով յիշատակներ--
բեկորներ միայն...

Ալ չեմ սիրեր ամառները
դուն հոս չես
դուն հոս չե՛ս:

17 Յունիս, 2008

1.

And so, it is the beginning of summer,
and you disappear
leaving me with memories,
morsels barely.

I don't like summers anymore
You're not here.
You're not *here*.

June 17, 2008

1.

Y es el principio del verano,
y desapareces
dejándome recuerdos,
bocados apenas.

Ya no me gustan los veranos
No estás aquí.
No estás *aquí*.

Junio 17, 2008

2.

Աշուն

Արեւոտ, նոյեմբերեան
Շողեր սենեակիս մէջ:

Հեռաձայնի կապեր մօտ ու հեռու
Սիրոյ ու բարեկամութեան փառատօներ:

Դուրսը դեղնորակ տերեւներ
Կը կտրտուին քայլերու տակ:

Կը նստիմ métro
ու կ'երթամ ու՞ր,

Ուր որ կամ ես՝ մի՛ւս կեանքիս մէջ.
Բայց ինչպէս ապրիմ հոս ԵՒ հոն:

Կը հասնիմ միւս կայարանը:
Վերջ երեւակայութեան:

Նոյեմբեր 12, 2006

2.

Fall

Sunny, November rays
in my room.

Phone calls from near and far
Love and friendship parades.

Outside, turning leaves
break under my steps.

I take the subway
to go to....

... that other life.
But how can I live in both places?

Arrival.
End of day dreams.

November 12, 2006

2.

Otoño

Rayos solares de noviembre
en mi alcoba.

Llamadas de cerca y de lejos
Desfiles de amor y de amistad.

Afuera, hojas cambiantes
se quiebran bajo mis pasos.

Tomo el subterráneo
para ir a....

... aquella otra vida.
¿Pero cómo vivir en ambos lugares?

Llegada.
Fin de los sueños diurnos.

Noviembre 12, 2006

3.

Երկու Անիներ

Արա Նիճիգեանի յիշատակին

Սեղանիս վրայ են
Անի քաղաքէն կաւէ կտորներ։

Դարերէ ի վեր կը սպասին
Որ հայ ձեռքեր հաւաքեն ու
Բերեն այս ափերուն սա իրերը։

Առաջին անգամ բռնեցի զանոնք ու ահա՛
Հեռուէն լուրե՛ր.
Ուրիշ Անի մը եւս կը կանգնի որբ ու քաշ։

5 Մայիս, 2007

3.

The Two Anis

                                          To *the memory of Ara Nuyujukian*

On the table
Clay pieces from ancient ANI*

Waiting for centuries for Armenian hands
to gather them and bring them to these shores…

I hold them for the first time and lo'
News from afar

Another Ani stands orphaned and courageous.

May 5, 2007

* *This was the capital of Armenia, around 1000 AD. It sits near the current Armenia/Turkish border. It is also used as a female personal name in modern Armenian.*

3.

Las Dos Anis

A la memoria de Ara Nuyujukian

Sobre la mesa
Trozos de cerámica de la antigua ANI*

Esperando siglos unas manos armenias
que los reúnan y los traigan a estas orillas...

Los sostengo por vez primera y advierto
Noticias de la lejanía

Otra Ani se yergue huérfana y valiente.

La capital Armenia, alrededor del año 1000 DC. Se ubica cerca de la frontera armenio-turca. También se usa como nombre femenino en la Armenia moderna.

4.

Թթենին
     Հերայն տարեդարձին առիթով

87րդ փողոցի հիւսիսային ափին
Երբ կը քալէի ՝ գտայ փոքրիկ պարտէզ մը.
Կ'աճապարէի բայց կեցայ ՝ ապշած
Հոն գտնուող թթենիին առջեւ։

Մարդիկ հոս հոն նստած ՝
Պարտէզին մէջ կը խօսէին, կը խնդային։
Մէկը չէր նկատեր կարծես ծառը
Իր երկար ճիւղերով, իր փոքրիկ տերեւներով
Որոնք շուք կը տարածէին
Նստարանի մը վրայ, շրջապատուած հասուն թութերով,
ոտնաքայլերու տակ ճզմուած։

Մէկը արդեօք որ մը նստա՞ծ էր հոն,
Քաղա՞ծ էր ափ մը թութ. կերա՞ծ էր.
Երազա՞ծ էր այդ նստարանին վրայ.
Նուիրա՞ծ բարի յիշատակներ
Մանկութենէն քաղած վայրկեաններ
Եւ կամ սիրահարի մը հետ նստած
Վի՞շտ մը՞, երա՞գ մը։

Յունիս 4, 2006

4.

The Mulberry Tree

To Hera, on her birthday

As I was walking on the north side of West 87th Street
I found a small garden.

Although I was in a rush, I stood
astonished to find a mulberry tree.

People were sitting here and there
in the garden, talking and laughing.
No one seemed to notice the tree
with its long branches and small leaves
shading a bench
surrounded by crushed ripe mulberries.

Had anyone sat there?
Picked a handful of berries? Tasted them?
Basked in happy thoughts?
Some remembrances of childhood?
Or shared a moment with a lover,
Recalling an anguish, a dream?

June 4, 2006

4.

La Morera

Para Hera, en su cumpleaños

Mientras caminaba al norte de la Calle 87 Oeste
encontré un pequeño jardín.

Aunque estaba de prisa, me detuve
sorprendida de encontrar una morera.

La gente se sentaba aquí y allá
en el jardín, hablando y riendo.
Nadie parecía notar el árbol
con sus largas ramas y pequeñas hojas
dando sombra a una banca
rodeada por maduras moras magulladas.

¿Estuvo alguien sentado allí?
¿Levantó una mano llena de moras? ¿Las probó?
¿Regodeándose con pensamientos felices?
¿Algunas evocaciones de la infancia?
¿O compartió un momento con un amante,
Recordando una angustia, un sueño?

Junio 4, 2006

5.

Ի յիշատակ մոռացութեան

«Օդը փոփոխամիտ է:»
Քեզ նման, հոգի՛ս:

Չիս ուզեցիր քշել մինչեւ դրախտ,
Բայց կէս ճամբան կեցար,
Թողնելով զիս ու Նանան
Մութ անապատին մէջ:

Ահա եօթը տարիներ անցա՛ծ,
Այդ անապատը պարտէզի վերածեցի:
Կանանչ խոտեր ծածկած են հետքերդ.
Ծաղիկներ պղտորած դիմագիծդ,
Վնասած յիշատակներս ու Նանայի մը փափաքը:

18 Յունիս 2007

5.

To the memory of forgetfulness

"The weather keeps changing!"
Like you, my love.

You wanted to take me to Paradise.
But mid-way you stopped, leaving me and Nana in the desert.

Seven years have passed
And the desert is now a garden:
Green grass has covered your steps,
Flowers have disguised your profile,
Leaving memories, and the wish of a Nana, behind.

June 18, 2007

5.

A la memoria del olvido

"¡El clima sigue cambiando!"
Como tú, amor mío.

Quisiste llevarme al Paraíso.
Pero a medio camino te detuviste, dejándome con Nana en el desierto.

Siete años han pasado
Y el desierto ahora es un jardín:
Verdes hierbas cubrieron tus huellas,
Flores disfrazaron tu perfil,
Dejando memorias, y el deseo de una abuela, atrás.

6.

Կեանք

Այս մէկը գործարանի մը մէջ մեռաւ քսանհինգ տարեկանին
Ուրիշ մը զինուոր, երրորդ մը կէթոյի մը մէջ նահատակ։
Կին մը շաբաթը եօթը օր կը սպասարկէ,
Քոյրը՝ ուրիշին զաւակները կը մեծցնէ։

Կեանքի հերոսներ՝
Ե՞րբ ձեր կարգին պիտ' հանգչիք,
Ո՞վ ձեր զաւակները կը մեծցնէ.
Ո՞վ ո՞վ ձեր մահը կու լայ։

2 Նոյեմբեր 2006

6.

LIFE (English version)

She dices the onions finely.
A construction worker, 25, falls to his death.

She adds the coriander, cloves and ginger.
A soldier, 21, walks over a roadside bomb.

She removes the meatballs from the fridge
A journalist, 43, gets shot thru the head.

She stirs the sauce over a low fire
and adds a few tears to the pot.

November 2, 2006

6.

Vida

Ella corta las cebollas finamente.
Un obrero de construcción, de 25 años, cae hacia su muerte.

Ella agrega cilantro, clavos y jengibre.
Un soldado, de 21 años, pisa una mina al borde del camino.

Ella saca las albóndigas de la nevera.
Un periodista, de 43 años, recibe un tiro en la cabeza.

Ella revuelve la salsa a bajo fuego
y añade algunas lágrimas a la olla.

Noviembre 2, 2006

7.

Նստած եմ երկրագունդին մէկ անկիւնը
Բայց կարծես գտնուիմ հիւսիսային Ափրիկէ:

Շուրջս կարմիր գորգեր, արմաւենիներ,
Խոհանոցէն համեղ բոյրեր...

Հոն կին մը իր champagne-ը կը կոնծէ
Դիմացի աթոռը դատարկ է.
Ի՞նչ կը տօնէ, եւ որո՞ւն կենացը կը խմէ:
Իր ազատութեա՞ն, այդ օրուան գեղեցիկ յիշատա՞կը,
զալիք գիշերուան այցելու՞ն,
Թէ սիրահարին մատներուն հետքը
իր վզին, ուսերուն վրայ:

14 Յունուար 2007

7.

I am sitting in this corner of the globe
but I could easily be in North Africa,
surrounded with red carpets and palm trees,
a delicious aroma permeating from the kitchen.

A lady sits nearby, gulping champagne,
an empty seat before her.
What is she celebrating, whose health is she drinking?
Her freedom, the end of a delightful day,
the visitor tonight, her lovers' fingers'
imprint on her neck, her shoulders?

January 14, 2007

7.

Me siento en esta esquina del mundo
pero podría fácilmente estar en el norte de África,
rodeada de alfombras rojas y palmeras,
mientras un delicioso aroma llega desde la cocina.

Una señora se sienta cerca, toma champaña,
un asiento vacío ante ella.
¿Qué celebra, a la salud de quién bebe?
¿Por su libertad, por el fin de un día encantador,
por el visitante nocturno, por los dedos de su amante
que marcan su cuello y sus hombros?

8.

Պոստոն՝ Ապրիլ 30, 2006

Մօրս պէժ քաշմիր բուրդը
Կեանքս ազատեց երբ հասայ
Ծանր հարբուխով մը:

Երանի՜ իմ կարգիս կարենայի
Կեանքը ազատել այն ընտանիքին
Որ հիւսեց այդ բուրդը:

Ո՞ւր է արդարութիւնը,
Մարդոց խի՞ղճը:

Հնդկաստան – Բագիստան – Քաշմիր – Պանկլատէշ:

8.

Boston, April 30, 2006

My mother's beige cashmere sweater
saved my life when I arrived
with a bad cold

I wish in return I could
save the lives of those
who wove that wool

Where is justice?
Human conscience?

India – Pakistan – Kashmir – Bangladesh

8.

Boston, Abril 30, 2006

El suéter beige de cachemira de mi madre
salvó mi vida cuando llegué
con un resfrío

Quisiera a cambio
salvar las vidas de aquellos
que tejieron esa lana

¿Dónde está la justicia?
¿Dónde la moralidad?

India - Pakistán - Cachemira - Bangladesh

9.

Անձրեւ

Կը քալեմ ծովափին
Ու դուն բացակայ ես.
Տուն մնացիր,
Չիս թողնելով բոպիկ
Աւազին հետ խաղալու:

Անձրեւին կաթիլները
Ուսերուս ու դէմքիս
Կը թմբկահարեն:

Երեկ երազիս մէջ
Արեւածագին երկու՛ր
Պտոյտէ մը կը վերադառնայի,
Անտառին մէջէն անցնելով:
Մշուշն ու ցօղը իրարու հետ կը խաղային:

Երբ պարտէզի դռնէն մտայ
Քու ժպիտդ ճառագայթեց սրտիս
Ու զիս ընդունեցիր
Գաւաթ մը սուրճ ձեռքիդ:

21 Ապրիլ 2007

9.

Rain

I am on the beach
And you are absent.
You stayed home
Letting me play
Alone with the sand.

The rain drops
drum on my face and shoulders.

I dreamt of you last night.
I was returning from a long walk
through the forest at dawn.
The dew was intertwined with the mist.

And when I walked in
you were like a sun's ray –
greeting me with
warmth, and care, and coffee.

April 21, 2007

9.

Lluvia

Estoy en la playa
Y tú no estás.
Permaneciste en casa
Dejándome jugar
Sola con la arena.

Las gotas de lluvia
golpean mi rostro y mis hombros.

Soñé contigo anoche.
Retornaba de una larga caminata
a través del bosque al amanecer.
El rocío estaba trenzado con la niebla.

Y cuando entré
Fuiste como un rayo de sol –
saludándome con
calidez y cuidado y café.

4/21/07

10.

Գիշերը՝ ցուցադրութենէն ետք

Ի՞նչ կը կարդաս.
Ինչու՞ կը կարդաս.
Ըսէ՛
Բացատրէ՛ այդ ծարաւը

Գիշերը կը քնանա՞ս։
Պատմէ՛ երազներդ, երաժշտութեամբ.
Նայիր – դէմքս կը ժպտի – քեզի համար։

Մայիս 12, 2006

10.

In the evening, after an exhibit

What are you reading?
Why do you read? Do tell!
Explain that thirst.

Do you sleep at night?
Tell me your dreams, with music.
See, I am smiling, for you.

May 12, 2006

10.

Al atardecer, después de una exposición

¿Qué estás leyendo?
¿Por qué lo lees? ¡Dilo!
Explica esa sed.

¿Duermes en la noche?
Cuéntame tus sueños, con música.
Mira, estoy sonriendo, para ti.

Mayo 2006

11.

Տաաը օր է կ'անցրեւէ

Երբեմն թուք մը, երբեմն տեղատարափ
Հասանք շաբաթ օր եւ նորէն
Հողը գեխի վերածեց այս լողանքը.

Մութ ամպեր
Թաց ուրքեր
Դէմքերը անժպիտ
Գարունը անվերջ։

6 Յունիս, 2009

11.

It's been raining for 10 days

Sometimes a mere spit, sometimes thundershowers
We've made it to Saturday, and once again
The pour has turned the ground to mud.

Dark clouds
Wet feet
Faces dim
Spring unending

June 6, 2009

11.

Llueve hace diez días

Algunas veces una simple escupa, otras veces tormentas eléctricas,
Nosotros hemos resistido hasta el sábado, y una vez más
El diluvio ha convertido la tierra en lodo.

Nubes oscuras
Pies húmedos
Rostros tenues
Primavera interminable

Junio 6, 2009

12.

Գալով անցեալին

Կը քալեմ յիշատակներուս հետ
Քայլ առ քայլ
Կանանչ լոյս յառա՛ջ
Կարմիր լոյս կա՛նգ:
Ա՛ջ, ձա՛խ, ա՛ջ, ձա՛խ
Շնչելով, աշխոյժ ապա՛ յոգնած:

Անցեալը պղտոր է.
Որու՞ մասին էր վերջին մտածումս.
Կլիման կարծես օգնեց:

Անձրեւ, անձրեւոտ է այսօր,
Կ'անձրեւէ՞ր այդ օրը, միթէ՞:
Այն՛ անձրեւանոց մը կար ձեռքիդ
Ես *անբրաց* հագած էի եւ
Կզակս թաց էր – կը յիշեմ:

Կանանչ լոյս յառա՛ջ
Կարմիր լոյս կա՛նգ

Եւ արդէն մայրը կտրեցի հանդիպման համար

Անձրեւանոցը մեծ էր եւ երկուքիս պաշտպան ...
բայց շուտով տեղատարափը դադրեցաւ։
Դէմքիդ ժպիտ մը կար։

Ա՛ջ, ձա՛խ, ա՛ջ, ձա՛խ
Չերք ձեռքի։
Դուն անձրեւանոցդ բռնած ու ես *անոռագով*.
քանի մը փողոց եւս
քանի մը վայրկեան եւս։

Կանանչ լոյս յառա՛ջ
Կարմիր լոյս կա՛նգ։

3 Դեկտեմբեր 2009

12.

Speaking of the Past

I walk in the company of my memories
Step by step,
Street by street.
Green light, go!
Red light, stop!
Right, left, right, left.
Breathing deeply, and then tired.

The past is getting dimmer.
Who was I thinking about a few minutes ago?
The weather seems to help me remember.

Rain, it's raining, today.
Was it raining on that day?
Yes, there was an umbrella with you
And I was wearing an anorak
And my chin was wet – I remember.

Green light, go!
Red light, stop!
And I cross the street for the meeting.

The umbrella was large and protected us both,
And soon the rain stopped. There was a smile on your face.

Right, left.

Right, left.
Hand in hand.

You're with your umbrella and I am wearing my anorak

A few more streets
A little while yet.
Green light, go!
Red light, stop!

December 2009

12.

Hablando del pasado

Camino en compañía de mis recuerdos
Paso a paso,
Calle a calle.
Luz verde, ¡adelante!
Luz roja, ¡detente!
Derecha, izquierda, derecha, izquierda.
Respiro hondamente, y luego me agoto.

El pasado se torna más oscuro.
¿En quién pensaba hace unos minutos?
El clima parece ayudarme a recordar.

Llueve, está lloviendo hoy.
¿Estuvo lloviendo aquel día?
Sí, tenías una sombrilla
Y yo tenía una chaqueta
Y mi mentón estaba húmedo – recuerdo.

Luz verde, ¡adelante!
Luz roja, ¡detente!
Y atravieso la calle para el encuentro.

La sombrilla era grande y nos protegía,
Y pronto la lluvia acabó. Había una sonrisa en tu rostro.

Derecha, izquierda.
Derecha, izquierda.
Mano en mano.

Estás con tu sombrilla y yo con mi chaqueta

Unas pocas calles más
Un poco más aún todavía.
Luz verde, ¡adelante!
Luz roja, ¡detente!

13.

Manifesto

Հայրս կ'ուզէր մեծ երաժիշտ ըլլայի
Եղայ երաժշտութիւնը սիրող։

Մօրաքոյրս *պալերին* է
Ու չեղայ պարող։
Բայց կը սիրեմ ՄԵՐԸ սիրոյն համար։

Եղբայրս լեզուաբան է
Ու ես լեզուները կը սիրեմ։

Մայրս գիտուն է
Ես խելացի կը փորձեմ ըլալ։

Բայց կը սիրեմ ԱՐՈՒԵՍՏԸ շունչի նման։

15 Մայիս, 2007

13.

Manifesto

Father wanted me to be a great musician
I became a music lover.

My aunt is a ballerina
I didn't become a dancer

But I love Love for the sake of love.

My brother is a multi-linguist
And I love languages

Mother is an intelligent woman
So I try to be wise

But I love Art like my own breath.

May 15, 2007

13.

Manifiesto

Mi padre quería que fuera una gran música
me convertí en una melómana.

Mi tía es una bailarina de ballet
Yo no me convertí en bailarina

Pero amo el AMOR por el amor.

Mi hermano es políglota
Y amo los idiomas

Mi madre es una mujer inteligente
Por tanto trato de ser sabia

Pero amo al ARTE como a mi propio aliento.

Mayo 15, 2007

14.

Տապանաքար

Մէկ ամիս է չե՛մ գրած.
Մէկ ամիս է չեմ սիրա՛ծ:

Երկու ամիս է չե՛մ խմած.
Երկու ամիս է չեմ քունա՛ծ:

Երեք ամիս է չե՛մ ուզած.
Երեք ամիս է չեմ նեղուա՛ծ:

3 Սեպտեմբեր, 2007

14.

Tombstone

It's been a month since I've written,
It's been a month since I've loved!

It's been two months since my last drink,
It's been two months since my last fuck!

It's been three months since I've wanted,
It's been three months since I've anguished!

September 3, 2007

14.

Lápida

Ha sido un mes desde que he escrito,
¡Ha sido un mes desde que he amado!

Han sido dos meses desde mi último trago,
¡Han sido dos meses desde mi última follada!

Han sido tres meses desde que he deseado,
¡Han sido tres meses desde que me he angustiado!

Septiembre 3, 2007

15.

Ձօն՝ Լոյսի ու Արեւի

Խուսափիմ պիտի սէրէ,
Յաւէ ու քեզմէ.
Երթամ հեռու ծառաստան՝
Դիտեմ սկիւռներն իրենց պարին մէջ,
Ծաղիկներն իրենց բոյրին մէջ,
Ամպերն ու արեւը իրենց ճամբուն վրայ.
Որոնք կարծես ուղիիս միշտ հակառակ են։

12 Մայիս, 1992

15.

Ode to Light and Sun

I shall escape from love, pain and you,
Travel to far away forests
Watch the squirrels in their dance
The flowers in their scent
The clouds and the sun on their way
Which seems to be the opposite to my journey.

May 12, 1992

15.

Oda a la luz y al sol

Escaparé del amor, del dolor y de ti,
Viajaré a lejanos bosques
Miraré las ardillas en su danza
Las flores en su esencia
Las nubes y el sol en su camino
Que parece ser el opuesto de mi viaje.

Mayo 12, 1992

16.

Մազերդ

Մոմին ու հովին խաղերը այս իրիկուն
Կը յիշեցնեն այն վայրկեանը երբ
Յօդ մը ցոլաց մազերուդ մէջ
Շուք մը – սեւ – մազերդ զանգուա́ր:

Ի ̊նչ օգուտ աչքերս «բաց» երազելէ.
Մեր վերջին հանդիպումը
Թափանցեց մինչեւ խորքս:

Արդեօք սու ̊տ մըն էր:

Բա́յց տեսա́յ շրթներուդ ժպիտը
Զգացի́ աչքերուդ փայլքը
Շօշափեցի́ հոգիդ որը
Փոթորկեց ներքին աշխարհս:

12 Յունիս 2006

16.

Your hair

The candle's shadow and the wind are playing games this evening
They remind me of the time when
A dew drop shined in your hair,
A shadow – black – your hair, full of curls.

But what good is it to dream with my eyes open.
Our last encounter
Penetrated my deepest being.

Was it a lie?

But I saw the smile on your lips,
I felt the glow of your eyes
I grazed your spirit
Which stirred my soul.

June 12, 2006

16.

Tu cabello

La sombra de la vela y el viento están jugando esta tarde
Me recuerdan el tiempo cuando
Una gota de rocío brillaba en tu cabello,
Una sombra – negra – tu cabello, lleno de rizos.

Pero qué bueno es soñar con mis ojos abiertos.
Nuestro último encuentro
Penetró mi ser más profundo.

¿Fue una mentira?

Pero vi la sonrisa en tus labios,
Sentí el brillo de tus ojos
Rocé tu espíritu
Que conmocionó mi alma.

Junio 12, 2006

17.

Գիշերը քունիս մէջ՝

Քրոշեան ընտանիքին՝ Պոստոն

Աշխարհը հանդարտ է,
Երկինքը անբիծ,
Քաղաքները լուռ
Փոքրիկները բարի
Պատանիները անկախ
Ծերերը ժպտուն
Աղքատները կուշտ
Հիւանդները յոյսով:

1 Յուլիս 2006

17.

As I sleep

                                      to the Kroshian family, Boston

The world is quiet
The sky – pure
The cities lie hushed
The kids are behaved
The elderly – smiling
The poor feel satiated
The sick full of hope.

July 1, 2006

17.

Mientras duermo

> A la familia Kroshian, en Boston

El mundo es silencioso
El cielo-puro
Las ciudades permanecen calladas
Los niños se comportan
Los ancianos sonríen
El pobre se siente saciado
El enfermo está lleno de esperanza.

Julio 1, 2006

18.

Լուսնակ գիշեր է,
Աստղեր կը փայլին
Փոքր օդանաւիս շուրջ.
արդեօ՞ք ճամբան կը լուսաւորեն որ ապահով հասնիմ։

Հոս հոն փոքր քաղաքներ
կը շողան ադամանդներու նման
ու ահա հորիզոնին՝
արեւը կը ծագի։

1 Յուլիս 2006

18.

It is a moonlit sky
The stars shine
Around my small plane;
Perhaps they are lighting the way so I may arrive safely?

Here and there small cities
Glow as if they were stars
And now, at the horizon
the Sun rises.

July 1, 2006

18.

Es un cielo iluminado por la luna
Las estrellas brillan
Alrededor de mi pequeño avión;
¿Tal vez iluminan para que pueda llegar sin peligro?

Aquí y allá pequeñas ciudades
Brillan como estrellas
Y ahora, en el horizonte
el sol despunta.

Julio 1, 2006

19.

Karaoke-ական անէծքներ
(Երեւանեան գիշերներ)

Կ'անիծեմ այդ   բառը,
                     Գաղափարը
                     Տանուտէրը այդ bar-ին։

Կը թքեմ երեսը   ստեղծողին՝
                     Գացողին՝
                     Երգողին՝
                     Առհասարակ խմողին։

Երազիս մէջ՝ ամպերու վրայ եմ,
                     Երկնցած
                     Հանգչած։

Սուրճի   բոյրը
                    Խառոյկը
                    Մութը
                    Հան/դար/տու/թիւնը։

21 Հոկտեմբեր, 2006

19.

Karaoke curses
(or Yerevan nights)

I curse that word
        Its idea
        The owner of that bar.

I spit at the face of its creator
        The patron
        The singer
        In general, the drinker.

In my dreams, I am on a bed of clouds
        Reclining
        Reposing.

The smell of coffee
        The woodfire
        The dark
        The C/A/L/M

October 21, 2006

19.

Maldiciones de karaoki
(o noches de Yerevan)

Maldigo   Esa palabra
    Su idea
    El dueño de ese bar.

Escupo   En el rostro de su creador
    El patrón
    El cantante
    En general, el bebedor.

En mis sueños,   Estoy sobre una cama de nubes
    Reclinándome
    Reposando.

El olor de   café
    La madera encendida
    La oscuridad
    La C/A/L/M/A

Octubre 21, 2006

20.

Կիրակի առտու՝

Սուրճի գաւաթներն արդէն դատարկ
Օխախոտն ու գռնյաբը սեղանին վրայ
Կը խօսակցին որ մոռնան
Յոգնութիւնն ու առանձնութիւնը։

Աղբահաւաքները բարձրաձայն ու արթուն են.
Մէկը չի նկատեր զիրենք
Երբ կը մեկնին շարունակելու իրենց գործը
Պարսելոնայի ուղիներու մէջ։

Ուրիշներ իրենց թերթը կը կարդան
Գարեջուրն ու նախաճաշը քովերնին.
Այլ մարդիկ ծխախոտ ծխած ատենին
Մտածումներու մէջ կը սպասեն քաղաքին շունչը։

Զբօսաշրջիկներ կը մօտենան
Յանկալով մտնել բայց դիմացի
Starbucks-ը տեսնելով կանգ կ'առնեն
Պատմական եկեղեցւոյ կից։

Նստած եմ ու կը ցանկամ այս մթնոլորտը
հետս տանիլ տուն։

25 մարտ 2007

20.

Sunday Morning

They sit between their shifts with their *café amb let*,
their cigarettes and the cognac,
Chatting away the stress, fatigue and loneliness.

The sweepers are loud and vivacious
Hardly noticed by the other patrons
as they leave to continue
with the pledge of *BC NETA!*

Others are reading their *País*
with their *croissant* and beer,
still others smoke contemplating the
Sunday hush the city exhales.

The tourists walk by wondering is
this the only café open near
Santa Maria Del Mar or is
Starbucks as good as the one back home?

I sit hoping to capture a little of this
to take home.

March 25, 2007

20.

Mañana de domingo

Entre sus turnos se sientan con su *café amb let*,
sus cigarillos y el coñac,
parloteando para quitarse el estrés, la fatiga y la soledad.

Los barrenderos son ruidosos y vivaces
Difícilmente advertidos por los otros patrones
mientras parten a continuar
con el compromise de BC NETA

Otros leen su País
con croissant y cerveza,
incluso otros fuman contemplando el
silencio del domingo la ciudad exhala.

Los turistas pasan preguntándose si es
este el único café cercano a
Santa Maria Del Mar o es
Starbucks tan bueno como el de regreso a casa?

Me siento esperando capturar un poco de esto
para llevar a casa.

Marzo 25, 2007

21.

I wore white…

I wore white at Hrant Dink's memorial
Because love is everlasting
Hope is immemorial
And thoughts reverberate eternally

March 5, 2007

21.

Escribí blanco

Usé blanco en el monumento a Hrant Dink
Porque el amor es eterno
La esperanza inmemorial
Y los pensamientos reverberan eternamente

22.

Six Balloons

Six happy balloons,
six orange balloons went uptown
to enjoy the New York Philharmonic in Central Park.

But it rained, in fact it stormed that evening.

The six happy balloons were quickly saddened,
their multicolored ribbons were stained,
they were bombarded by rain drops.

So they went home, scarred.
One didn't make it through the night,
two others wouldn't stay aloft.

And, on day two, there were none.

July 14, 2007

22.

Seis globos

Seis globos felices,
seis globos naranja fueron a los suburbios a disfrutar
la Filarmónica de Nueva York en el Central Park.

Pero llovió, de hecho diluvió aquella tarde.

Los seis globos felices
se entristecieron rápido, sus cintas multicolores se mancharon,
bombardeadas por gotas de lluvia.

Entonces se fueron a casa, marcados;
Uno no logró pasar la noche, los otros dos no podían mantenerse
a flote.

Y al segundo día, no había ninguno.

Julio 14, 2007

23.

Vin Santo -- sweet wine
made of white ripe grapes.

Dip those biscotti. Finish it off with that espresso *doppio macchiato*.

Transport yourself to Florence,
or some tiny Tuscan village like San Giminiano, where the
medieval towers cast the only shadows *this* side of Sienna.

Think of all the people before you, who have admired the
paintings at the Uffizi;
Of all the people who have prayed at Santa Croce;
Of all those who hoped one day to see portraits hidden since
WWII in the underground tunnels.

Then thank the spirits who transported you there, as part of the
continuum called Humanity.
Thank your art teachers,
your parents, your lover,
whomever.

Just be thankful.

1/17/07

23.

Vino Santo – dulce vino
Hecho de blancas uvas maduras.

Remoja aquellas galletas --
pásalas completamente con aquel espresso doppio macchiato.

Transpórtate a Florencia --
o a alguna diminuta aldea toscana como San Giminiano,
donde las torres medievales
proyectan las únicas sombras a ESTE lado de Siena.

Piensa en toda la gente que antes de ti, admiró
estas pinturas en la Galería Uffizi;
en todos aquellos que han orado en la Santa Croce;
en todos aquellos que esperaron algún día ver
retratos escondidos en subterráneos desde la Segunda Guerra Mundial.

Luego agradece a los espíritus que te transportaron allí, como parte del continuo llamado Humanidad;
agradece a tus profesores de arte,
a tus padres,
a tu amante,
a cualquiera.

Sólo agradece.

1/17/07 NYC

24.

Three cups of Heaven

It was John who mentioned it first: *I've discovered Saffron Tea*, he said. And was quite determined that it should be *subtle*.

Tea is black, he added, *just as wine is red*. I couldn't agree more.

Patty came in with a care package that had IRAN stamped all over it:
bags of prepared Saffron tea
250 grams of *exported Isfahani Mirzapore*
green cardamom barely dried
and, a package of saffron you can't buy *this* side
of the Atlantic.

Saffron, the other gold.

I poured the water in the pot, added the tea, the pods and the magic powder, and drank three heavenly cups.

January 6, 2007

24.

Tres tazas de cielo

Fue John quien lo mencionó primero:
"Descubrí el té de azafrán", dijo.
Y estuvo muy determinado a que podría ser "suave".

"El té es negro", agregó, "así como el vino es rojo."
Yo no podría estar más de acuerdo.

Patty entró con un paquete estampado con IRÁN
en todas partes:
bolsas preparadas de té de azafrán, 250 gramos de Isfahani Mirzapore exportado
directamente desde IIIIIIIIRAAAAN,
cardamomo verde apenas seco, y un paquete de azafrán
que no puedes comprar a este lado
del Atlántico.

Azafrán, el otro oro.
Vertí el agua en la olla, agregué el té, las vainas
y el mágico poder, y bebí tres tazas celestiales.

Enero 6, 2007

25.

My new bookcases will arrive in a week

I empty the old ones and find among deposits of fine dust,
Layers of me at twenty, at twenty-five…

A copy of *100 Years of Solitude* in French,
A collection of science-fiction entrenched around copies of Voltaire.

Then notes in old travel books.
Some souvenirs bought or found.

Cookbooks with recipes of curry, *hamam meshwi*,
Grandmother's lentil soup and Mum's *mujjadarah*,

As I meander through them, I smile at my Present,
knowing that it and the Future have a solid Past.

12/23/07

25.

Mis nuevas bibliotecas llegarán en una semana

Desocupo las viejas y encuentro entre depósitos de fino polvo,
Capas de mí a los veinte, a los veinticinco años...

Una copia de *100 Años de Soledad* en francés,
Una colección de ciencia ficción atrincherada alrededor de
ejemplares de Voltaire.

Luego notas en viejos libros de viaje.
Algunos recuerdos comprados o encontrados.

Libros de cocina con recetas de curry, *hamam meshwi*,
La sopa de lentejas de la abuela y el *mujjadarah* de mamá,

Mientras hurgo entre ellos, sonrío a mi presente,
sabiendo que él y el futuro tienen un sólido pasado.

12/23/07

26.

Music

Close your eyes and think cha-cha-cha;
close your eyes and think of me
swaying left to right
to the rhythm.

Close your eyes and imagine me.

Dec 7, 2006

26.

Música

Cierra tus ojos y piensa en cha-cha-cha;
cierra tus ojos y piensa en mí
meneándome de derecha a izquierda
al ritmo de la música.

Cierra tus ojos e imagíname.

Diciembre 7, 2006

27.

Անո՛նք մեռան

Անո՛նք մեռան, հայր մայր ու դուստր
Ու թերթերը գրեցին
Բայց քանի՜ քանի՜ ուրիշներ մեռան
Առանձին

Զանոնք սպաննեցին, հայր մայր որդիններ
ու դրացիները տեսան
Բայց քանի՜ քանի՜ ուրիշներ սպաննուեցան
Առանձին

Զանոնք այրեցին, քույր եւ եղբայր
Ու ծնողները տեսան
Բայց քանի՜ քանի՜ քույրեր ու եղբայրներ
Այրեցան առանձին...

Զանոնք թաղեցին, հայեր, քիրտեր,
Արաբներ, ուրիշ ազգեր
Բայց քանի՜ քանի՜ ուրիշներ թաղուեցան
Առանց վկայի։

May 22, 2010

27.

They died

They died, father, mother and daughter
And the newspapers reported it
But how many others died
Alone.

They were killed, father, mother and children
And the neighbors witnessed it
But how many others were killed
Alone.

They were burned, sister and brother
And the parents saw it
But how many sisters and brothers
Were burnt, alone.

They were buried, Armenians, Kurds
Arabs, other peoples
But how many others were buried
Without a witness.

May 22, 2010

27.

Murieron

Murieron, padre, madre e hija
Y los periódicos lo reportaron
Pero cuántos más murieron
Solos.

Fueron asesinados, padre, madre e hijos
Y los vecinos lo atestiguaron
Pero cuántos más fueron asesinados
Solos.

Fueron quemados hermana y hermano
Y los padres lo vieron
Pero cuántos más
hermanas y hermanos
Fueron quemados, solos

Fueron enterrados, armenios, kurdos
Arabes, otras gentes
Pero cuántos más fueron enterrados
Sin testigo.

Traducción de Pamela Ospina

www.ingramcontent.com/pod-product-compliance
Lightning Source LLC
Chambersburg PA
CBHW051710040426
42446CB00008B/804